My First Counting Book

Compiled by Hugh Kingsley
Illustrated by Peter Kingston

Before they go to school, children need to have acquired the basics of the skills of reading, writing and counting. This preschool activity book introduces children to the world of numbers in an entertaining way. Parents' notes, at the bottom of each page, provide suggestions and further ideas for you to help your child acquire first counting skills, and to develop other skills too.

By using this book, children will learn to recognise numbers from 1 to 20 and learn to count; improve their hand–eye co-ordination and hand control by copying numbers (start at the arrows) and colouring; and with plenty to talk about, improve their powers of observation and their thinking and conversational skills as well. The Great River Race will give your child and his friends plenty of counting practice without them realising it!
Use a topic to introduce lots of other ideas: shapes, colours, opposites, and especially things that your child has experience of – going on holiday or visiting the shops, for example.

Some children prefer to use their left hand and may draw the numbers in a different way from right-handed children, but that's perfectly all right. To avoid the repetition of him/her, him is used throughout.

AWARD PUBLICATIONS LIMITED

1

The monkey is peeling one banana.
Which other kinds of fruit can you see?
How many of each can you count?

Copy the number 1 by joining up the dots. Practise writing more number 1s in the space alongside.

Play a game of I-spy. Look for single objects in the home – toys for example. How many of each can your child see? Ask him to join the dots and to colour in the banana to complete the picture.

1 2 3 4 5 6 7 8 9 10

There are two cars and two buses. How many people are in the red car and how many people are in the green car? Draw a driver in each bus.

2

Copy the number 2 by joining up the dots. Practise writing more number 2s in the space alongside.

Are the buses that run in your area different colours from those in the picture? Do you have a car? What colour is it? How many drivers can you see in the cars?

11 12 13 14 15 16 17 18 19 20

3

There are three children. How many of each kind of toy can you count? Draw lines to join up each of the teddy bears.

Copy the number 3 by joining up the dots. Practise writing more number 3s in the space alongside.

Choose up to three of each kind of your child's toys. Ask him to put them in groups and to count how many are in each group.

1   2   3   4   5   6   7   8   9   10

Four seals are having fun on the ice.
Look at all the animals swimming in
the water. Count the number of fishes.

4

**Copy the number 4 by joining up the dots. Practise
writing more number 4s in the space alongside.**

What do you think seals like to eat? Draw a line from each seal to
something he wants to eat. Do you know the names of the animals in
the water?

11 12 13 14 15 16 17 18 19 20

5

There are five zebras in the picture. Which other kinds of animal can you see? Count how many there are of each kind.

Copy the number 5 by joining up the dots. Practise writing more number 5s in the space alongside.

These animals all live in hot countries. Do you have any books with pictures showing where the animals live in the wild?

1 2 3 4 5 6 7 8 9 10

There are six yachts on the water. Count the number of yachts with red sails. What can you see on the shore nearby?

6

Copy the number 6 by joining up the dots. Practise writing more number 6s in the space alongside.

Yachts are sailed for fun but also in races. Small ones keep close to the shore. Ask your child to colour the white yachts and the white sail.

11 12 13 14 15 16 17 18 19 20

7

The table is laid ready for a birthday party. How many children will be there? Count the plates, tumblers, spoons and straws.

Copy the number 7 by joining up the dots. Practise writing more number 7s in the space alongside.

7

Most children love parties. They like talking about them, the games they play, the presents, and their friends! It's an ideal opportunity to start talking about relationships. Someone's lit the candles too soon!

1 2 3 4 5 6 7 8 9 10

The ski course is marked out with eight coloured flags. Count the number of fir-trees. How many skiers are on the course?

8

Copy the number 8 by joining up the dots. Practise writing more number 8s in the space alongside.

Lots of people take skiing holidays. Talk about holidays, mountains, snow, cold temperatures, warm ski clothes and bright colours. Can you see the snowboarder?

11 12 13 14 15 16 17 18 19 20

9

The nine rabbits can't believe there is so much food. What kinds of vegetables are there? How many of each kind can you see?

Copy the number 9 by joining up the dots. Practise writing more number 9s in the space alongside.

9

Where do rabbits live? What are their homes called? Does your child have a pet rabbit? Perhaps he has another kind of pet. Having a pet helps a child to learn to care for and share with others.

1 2 3 4 5 6 7 8 9 10

The children have picked ten apples and placed them in their basket. How many apples are left on the tree?

10

Copy the number 10 by joining up the dots. Practise writing more number 10s in the space alongside.

There are lots of different kinds of apples. Apples are grown on fruit farms in orchards. What other sorts of fruits are there? Look at all the different kinds of fruit next time you take your child to the supermarket.

11 12 13 14 15 16 17 18 19 20

11

The frog has eleven leaves on which to hop across the pond. Colour them to match those at the side of the pond.

Copy the number 11 by joining up the dots. Practise writing more number 11s in the space alongside.

11

Ponds attract wildlife. Apart from frogs what other sorts of animals and plants live there? Help your child to learn about protecting plants and animals.

1   2   3   4   5   6   7   8   9   10

There are twelve flowers in the border.
Count the number of flowers of each
colour. Colour in the stones in the path.

12

**Copy the number 12 by joining up the dots. Practise
writing more number 12s in the space alongside.**

The bright colours of flowers and their scents attract insects like butterflies
and honey-bees. Talk about other helpful insects that you find in the garden
— ladybirds, for instance — and the colours, shapes and sizes of flowers.

11 12 13 14 15 16 17 18 19 20

13

The diesel engine is pulling thirteen trucks. Count the number in each group loaded with different goods.

Copy the number 13 by joining up the dots. Practise writing more number 13s in the space alongside.

13

Railways still carry a lot of freight. Has your child seen a freight train? Is he more familiar with huge articulated vehicles? Perhaps he has some toys – a train or a big truck?

1 2 3 4 5 6 7 8 9 10

Passengers fly in aircraft all over the world. There are fourteen windows in the aeroplane. Count the people on the plane.

14

Copy the number 14 by joining up the dots. Practise writing more number 14s in the space alongside.

Has your child ever visited an airport or travelled by air? Talk about all the things that go on at a modern airport. Look at pictures of aircraft in other books.

11 12 13 14 15 16 17 18 19 20

15

The farmer has rounded up fifteen sheep with his sheepdog. Count the sheep with horns. How many have no horns?

Copy the number 15 by joining up the dots. Practise writing more number 15s in the space alongside.

15 15

Sheep provide meat to eat and wool to keep us warm. What other kinds of animal live on a farm? Talk to your child about how life in the country differs from life in the town.

1 2 3 4 5 6 7 8 9 10

There are sixteen seats on the rollercoaster. Count the people riding on it. How many empty seats can you see?

16

Copy the number 16 by joining up the dots. Practise writing more number 16s in the space alongside.

16 16

Has your child sever been to a funfair? It's not safe for young children to ride on a rollercoaster but usually there are lots of rides that are safe for preschool children and children just starting school.

11 12 13 14 15 16 17 18 19 20

17

There are seventeen items of clothing on the clothes-line. Count the number of items of each colour.

Copy the number 17 by joining up the dots. Practise writing more number 17s in the space alongside.

17 17

Washdays are favourites with many young children. Ask your child to name the items hanging on the line. Count the items as you put them into the washing-machine or hang them out to dry.

1 2 3 4 5 6 7 8 9 10

The pond has eighteen birds on and around it. Count the ducks. What are the pink birds called?

18

Copy the number 18 by joining up the dots. Practise writing more number 18s in the space alongside.

Do you have a pond nearby? Children enjoy watching water birds, especially ducks. Encourage your child to count the birds of each kind and to remember their names. Look at their colours and sizes.

11 12 13 14 15 16 17 18 19 20

19

Nineteen runners have just set off on the cross-country race. Count the runners who are wearing vests of each colour.

Copy the number 19 by joining up the dots. Practise writing more number 19s in the space alongside.

19

Has your child ever watched a race outdoors or on the television? Introduce him to the idea of athletes of different nationalities competing. Help him to learn the vest colours of different competitors.

1 2 3 4 5 6 7 8 9 10

Bees collect nectar when they visit flowers. Twenty bees fly back to the hive to make honey. Count the jars of honey.

20

Copy the number 20 by joining up the dots. Practise writing more number 20s in the space alongside.

Talk about bees and where they live. Watch bees in the garden as they fly from flower to flower. Which colours do they prefer?

11 12 13 14 15 16 17 18 19 20

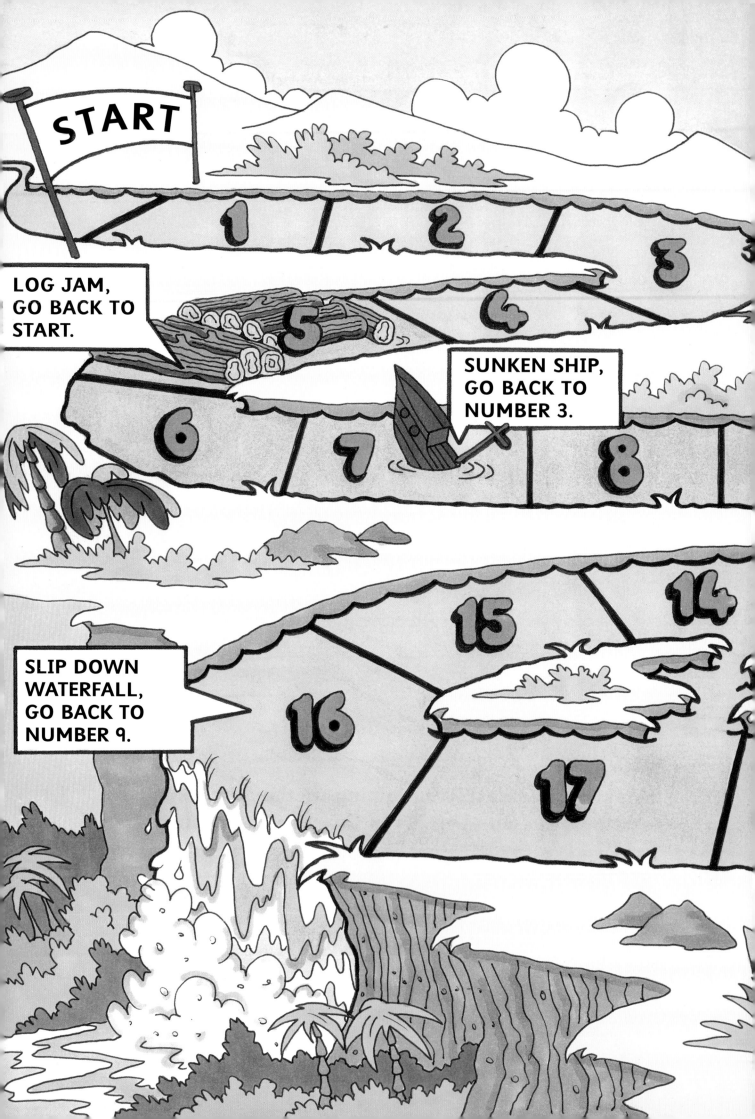

Animals Galore

Do you know the names of any of the animals in the picture? Count all the animals. How many can you see? How many wild animals are there? Count the farm animals. How many animals have horns?